The Usborne Little Book of Stories from the Old Testament

For Charlotte on the
occasion of her
christening 25/12/12.
from the Tulloch family
with love.

First published in 2007 by Usborne Publishing Ltd.
83-85 Saffron Hill, London EC1N 8RT, England.
www.usborne.com. Copyright © 2000, Usborne
Publishing Ltd. The name Usborne and the devices
♀ ⊕ are Trade Marks of Usborne Publishing Ltd. All
rights reserved. No part of this publication may
be reproduced, stored in a retrieval system, or
transmitted in any form or by any means,
electronic, mechanical, photocopying,
recording or otherwise, without the prior
permission of the publisher. First published
in America in 2008.
Printed in Dubai.

The Usborne Little Book of Stories from the
Old Testament

Retold by Heather Amery

Illustrated by Linda Edwards

Designed by Amanda Barlow

Edited by Jenny Tyler

Contents

How the World Began

Long, long ago, there was no world, no sky, no sun or stars, not even any day or night. There was only swirling water in a huge dark empty space. Then God made light and this was the very first day.

On the second day, God made the sky. Under the sky was nothing but water. God collected the water together to make the seas. Between the seas was dry land. God then ordered all kinds of plants and trees to grow on the land. That was the third day.

The next day, God put the sun in the sky to shine during the day and the moon to shine at night. On the fifth day, God said that all kinds of creatures should swim in the seas and all kinds of birds should fly in the sky. He blessed them, told them to have their

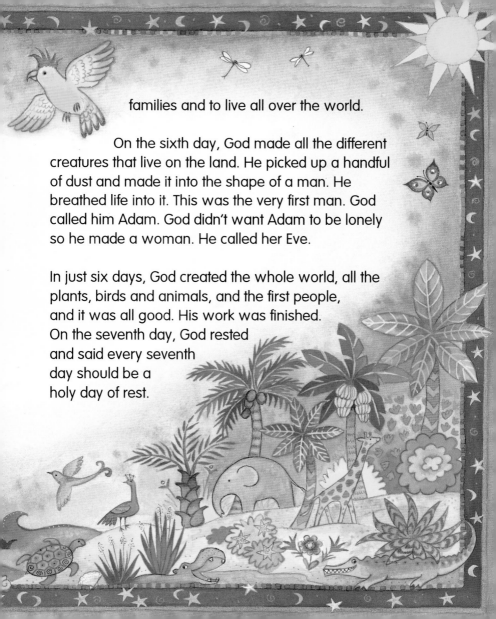

families and to live all over the world.

On the sixth day, God made all the different creatures that live on the land. He picked up a handful of dust and made it into the shape of a man. He breathed life into it. This was the very first man. God called him Adam. God didn't want Adam to be lonely so he made a woman. He called her Eve.

In just six days, God created the whole world, all the plants, birds and animals, and the first people, and it was all good. His work was finished. On the seventh day, God rested and said every seventh day should be a holy day of rest.

Adam and Eve

Adam and Eve lived in a beautiful garden God made specially for them. It was full of flowers and fruit trees. God told Adam he could eat the fruit from any of the trees, except the ones that grew on the Tree of Knowledge of Good and Evil. If he ate that, he would die.

Adam and Eve were very happy in the garden. There were sparkling rivers and every kind of animal and bird. Adam and Eve made friends with them all. Sometimes, God walked in the garden with Adam and Eve on warm summer evenings and talked to them.

A snake lived in the Garden. One sleepy afternoon, it slithered up to Eve and whispered in her ear. "Did God say you could eat the fruit of all the trees?" it asked.

"Yes," replied Eve, "except the fruit on the Tree of Knowledge in the middle of the Garden. If we touch or eat those, we shall die."

"You won't die," whispered the snake. "God knows that if you do eat it, you will become as wise as gods."

Eve walked slowly to the special tree. The fruit looked delicious. She picked one and took a big bite out of it. When Adam came up, she gave him the rest of the fruit to eat.

Then Adam and Eve looked at each other and saw for the first time that they had no clothes on. They felt very shy. They rushed away and sewed leaves together to make clothes before they could look at each other again.

That evening, God walked in the Garden. "Adam," He called, "where are you?"

"I'm here. I'm hiding from you because I know now that I was naked," said Adam.

"How do you know? Have you eaten the fruit I told you not to touch?" asked God.

"Eve gave it to me," said Adam.

"Why did you disobey me?" God asked Eve.

"The snake told me to," said Eve.

"Because you have disobeyed me, you must leave my Garden," said God. "You will have to work hard to grow food. The ground will be rough and stony and full of thorns and thistles. And when you grow old, you will die."

God watched Adam and Eve go out of the Garden. They had to begin their new, hard life on Earth. They were very miserable.

God sent an angel with a flaming sword to guard the Garden of Eden so that no one could ever go into it again.

11

Noah and his Ark

After many years, God looked at the world he had made and was sad. The people were bad, they hurt each other and did not listen to Him any more. God decided to flood the whole world so that everybody in it would drown.

There was just one man who loved God and obeyed Him. His name was Noah. God said to Noah, "You must build an ark, a huge boat, so I can save your family and all the creatures on Earth. I will tell you exactly how big it must be."

Noah did what God told him. He cut down trees and collected all the things he needed. Then he began to build his ark. His three sons helped him. They marked out the shape of the ark on the ground and made a wooden frame. Then they covered it with wood and put tar on the inside and outside to make the ark waterproof.

After months and months of hard work, it was finished. It had three decks, a door in the side and a roof, just as God had told Noah to build it. Noah and his family loaded the ark with food and water for themselves and for all the creatures.

Just as they were carrying on the last load, huge clouds drifted across the sky, blocking out the sun. Noah looked up and a few drops of rain fell on his head. Then he looked toward the hills. A huge procession of creatures was walking, trotting, creeping, slithering or flying in an endless line. There were two of every kind of animal and bird in the world. Noah stared at them. "I didn't know there were so many," he said. As he watched, they filed into the ark. There was just enough room for them all. Noah and his wife and his three sons and their wives went in too, and God closed the door after them.

Then it began to rain. It rained and rained for forty days and nights. Slowly the water flooded the ground and the ark floated away on a huge new sea, with everyone safely inside.

Outside, the water rose until it covered the very tops of the mountains, and everybody and everything left on the Earth was drowned in the flood.

For months and months the ark tossed on the waves of a huge empty sea. At last, the rain stopped and the water began to go down a little. Noah opened a window and sent off a raven. "Go and find some dry land," he said. The raven flew a very long way but it couldn't find any dry land.

Later Noah sent off a dove. It flew away but came back again. Noah waited a week and sent the dove off again. This time, it came back with a twig in its beak. "That means there is dry land and things are growing again," said Noah.

After another week, he sent off the dove again but, this time, it didn't come back. Noah lifted off a cover on the ark and looked out. At last, he could see land. Noah opened the door of the ark, and everyone rushed out. The land was dry and the sun was shining.

"Spread out all over the Earth and have your families," God said to Noah and to all the creatures.

Noah looked up and thanked God for saving them from the terrible flood. In the sky was a rainbow. "That is my sign," said God. "I promise I will never flood the whole Earth again."

16

Abraham and Sarah

Abraham was a rich man who lived in the city of Haran with his wife Sarah. They were both old and, to their great sadness, had never had any children.

One day, God said to Abraham, "I want you to go to the land of Canaan. There I will make you the father of a great nation."

Abraham didn't understand what God meant, but he always did what God told him to do. Soon he started out for Canaan with Sarah, his nephew Lot and his wife, and all his servants and his herds of sheep and goats. It was a very long journey but, at last, they reached the new land and put up their tents.

At first there was plenty of grass and water for Abraham's herds of sheep and goats and for Lot's herds as well. But, as the years passed, the herds grew bigger and bigger and there wasn't enough food for them all.

"It's time for us to part," Abraham said to Lot. "You can choose where you want to go."

"I'll go down to the valley. There's plenty of good grass and water there," said Lot.

"I'll stay here on the hills," said Abraham, although he knew the food and water wasn't so good. Lot and his wife said goodbye to Abraham and Sarah and led their sheep down to the valley. God again promised Abraham that He would make his family into a great nation.

One hot afternoon some years later, when Abraham was sitting in his tent, he saw three men crossing the hills. When they came nearer, he went to meet them.

"Come to my tent," Abraham said to the strangers. "You can wash and rest there, and have a meal."

Sarah and the servants made fresh bread, roasted some meat on the fire and gave the three men bowls of milk and cheese. When the feast was over, one of the men said, "We have a message from God for you.

You and Sarah will have a baby boy."

"We're both much too old to have children," laughed Sarah. But the months went by and Sarah gave birth to a son. She called him Isaac. Abraham and Sarah were delighted that they had a child at last. And Abraham remembered that God had told him he would be the father of a great nation.

Isaac and Rebecca

Isaac, the son of Abraham and Sarah, grew up a strong and tall young man. Sarah had died and Abraham decided it was time for Isaac to have a wife. But it had to be a girl from their own people who lived far away from Canaan.

Abraham said to a servant, "Go to my brother Nahor to choose a wife for Isaac and bring her here."

"If she doesn't want to come, shall I take Isaac to her?" asked the man.

"No, Isaac must stay here. God promised this land to my family,"

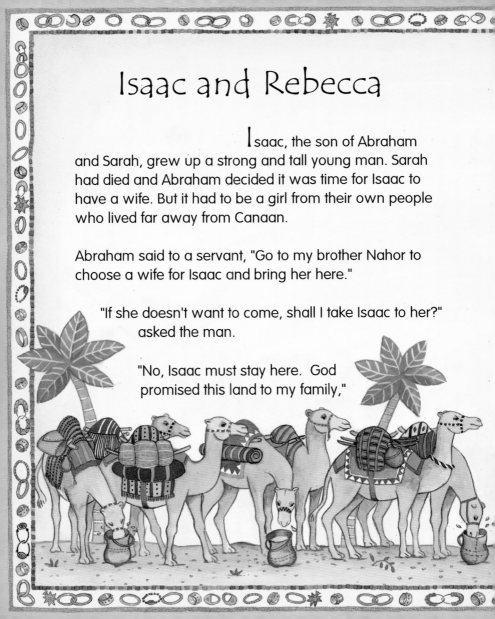

said Abraham. "She must come and live with us here."

The servant began his long journey with some other servants, taking ten camels and presents for the girl and her family. At last he stopped at a well outside the city walls. It was late in the afternoon and soon the girls would come to the well to fill their water jars.

The servant said a prayer to God. "Please help me find a wife for Isaac. I'll say to one of the girls, 'Please give me a drink from your water jar.' If she says, 'Yes, and I will also give water to your camels,' let her be the right wife for Isaac."

Before he finished his prayer, the servant looked up and saw a beautiful girl

walking to the well. After she had filled her jar, he asked for water. She gave him the jar and, after he had a long drink, she filled her jar again and again with water for his camels.

The servant knew this was the sign he had prayed for. He gave the girl a gold ring and two gold bracelets. "Tell me who you are," he said. "May we spend the night in your father's house?"

"My name is Rebecca and my grandfather's name is Nahor. We have plenty of room for you and food for your camels," said the girl.

The servant thanked God for leading him straight to Abraham's family.

Rebecca ran to her house. She told her family about the man she had met at the well and showed them the presents he had given her. Laban, her brother, went back to the well and asked the servant and other men to come to the house.

After the camels were fed for the night, everyone sat down to a good meal. But the servant would not start eating until he had told Rebecca's family why he had come.

He told them about Abraham and Sarah and their son, Isaac, and how he had asked God to help him choose the right girl at the well. Then he asked her family if they would let Rebecca go back to Canaan with him to be Isaac's wife.

Rebecca's family saw it was the will of God and agreed that Rebecca should go. Abraham's servant gave presents of jewels to Rebecca and presents to her mother and brother. Then they feasted to celebrate the engagement.

Abraham's servant wanted to go home at once and Rebecca agreed to go with him. The next morning, the men loaded up the camels. Rebecca said goodbye to her family and began the long journey to Canaan.

It was evening when, at last, they reached Abraham's tent. Isaac was out in the fields and saw the camels coming. He went to meet them and the servant told him everything that had happened. Isaac looked at the beautiful girl who had come so far to be his bride. He soon married her, and he loved her.

Joseph and his Wonderful Coat

Jacob, Isaac's son, was a rich farmer who lived in Canaan. He had twelve sons and, although he loved them all, he loved his son Joseph most of all. He gave Joseph a wonderful coat. Joseph strutted around in it, thinking himself very grand. His brothers were jealous. They hated him because Joseph said he dreamed he would be much more important than them.

One day, Jacob sent Joseph out to a far valley to his brothers and their flocks of sheep and goats. When his brothers saw Joseph coming, one said, "Let's kill him. We could tell our father that a wild animal has eaten him."

But another brother said, "We mustn't kill him. Let's put him into that pit." Just then, some merchants passed by on their way to Egypt. The brothers sold Joseph to them as a slave and the merchants led him away. The brothers put goat's blood on Joseph's coat and went home to their father.

"We found this coat. Is it Joseph's?" one brother asked him. Jacob recognized the coat and, when he saw the blood on it, he thought Joseph was dead. He was very sad.

The merchants took Joseph to Egypt and sold him as a slave to Potiphar, the captain of the King's guard. Joseph worked hard and soon Potiphar put him in charge of his household. For a time, all went well, but Potiphar's wife wanted to make trouble for Joseph. She told Potiphar, "That Joseph has been very rude to me."

It wasn't true, but Potiphar was angry with Joseph. He had him put in prison. God had made Joseph very good at telling people what their dreams meant and he explained the other prisoners' dreams to them.

After Joseph had been in prison for two years, the King of Egypt had a strange dream. He asked his wise men what it meant, but no one could explain it. Then someone remembered that Joseph was good at dreams. He was brought to the King. The King told Joseph his dream.

Joseph said, "Your dream means that for seven years there will be good harvests with lots of food for everyone. But then there will be seven years when the harvests are bad and many people will be hungry, even starving."

The King was so pleased with Joseph, he put him in charge of all the stores of food in Egypt. For seven years, there were good harvests and Joseph made sure the extra grain was stored away. When the seven bad years came, Joseph had plenty of food to sell to the people.

Far away in Canaan, Joseph's father and brothers grew short of food. Jacob said, "You must go to Egypt to buy grain. They have plenty". Ten brothers began the journey, leaving the youngest, Benjamin, behind.

In Egypt, the brothers asked the governor if they could buy food. They didn't know he was their brother Joseph, but Joseph knew at once they were his brothers. He spoke sternly and asked them about their father and Benjamin.

He said, "I'll sell you food but when you come again, you must bring Benjamin with you. I'll keep your brother Simeon here until you come back."

The brothers started for home. On the way, they opened the sacks of grain they had bought and found the money they had paid to Joseph. They were very frightened. "God is punishing us for selling Joseph," the brothers said. They didn't know Joseph had told his servants to put it there.

After a while, Jacob and his sons had eaten all the grain. They had to go back to Egypt to buy more, but this time they took Benjamin with them. Again, they asked Joseph to sell them food and still they didn't know he was their brother. Joseph ordered his servants to give them a meal, making sure Benjamin had plenty to eat.

The next morning, the eleven brothers started for home.

On the way, Joseph's guards caught up with them and opened the sacks of grain. In Benjamin's sack was Joseph's silver cup. Joseph had told his guards to hide it there. He wanted to test his brothers.

The guards marched the scared brothers back to Egypt and took them to Joseph. "You may go home," he said, "but you must leave Benjamin here with me."

The brothers were very upset. "Please let us take Benjamin with us," they begged. "Our father has already lost one son. If he loses Benjamin, it will break his heart. Let one of us stay here instead of Benjamin." Joseph knew then that his brothers had changed and were sorry for what they had done to him long ago.

"I am Joseph, your brother whom you sold as a slave," Joseph cried. "But it was God who sent me to Egypt so that I could save you from dying of hunger. God promised Abraham that the nation he founded would be safe. Go back to my father and bring him here, with all your family and your animals. I will give you good land and we will all live well and happily in Egypt."

Moses in the Bulrushes

Many years after Joseph died, Egypt had a new King who was very cruel to Joseph's family, the Hebrews, who lived in Egypt. He made them work as slaves. They were forced to make bricks of mud to build great cities and temples for the King and to work on the land.

The Hebrews worked hard from early morning until late at night, watched over by Egyptian guards, and they were beaten if they tried to rest.

There were so many Hebrews in Egypt by this time that the King was frightened they would rebel against him and seize his throne. So he made a new law and ordered his soldiers to kill all the Hebrew baby boys as soon as they were born.

One Hebrew mother managed to hide her new baby son, called Moses, until he was three months old. But as he grew older, she was afraid the Egyptian soldiers would hear him crying, find him and then kill him.

One day, she picked up Moses and hurried secretly
down to the river bank. There she made a basket out of
reeds and covered the outside with tar to make it
waterproof. When the basket was finished, she put Moses
in it. He was fast asleep. She put the basket gently down
on the water and pushed it out on the great Nile river.

Moses's sister was hiding in the reeds. She watched the
basket float away down the river. She followed it, walking
along the bank to see where it would go.

A little farther along the bank, the Egyptian Princess came
down to the river to swim with her servants. She saw the

basket floating on the water between
the reeds.

"Bring that basket here," she ordered one of her maids.
The maid picked up the basket and brought it to her.

When the Princess saw the baby, she said, "That must be
a Hebrew boy." At that moment, Moses woke up and
cried a little. The Princess felt so sorry for him, she
decided to keep him.

Moses's sister watched, hidden in the reeds.

She saw what happened. She ran to the Princess. "Do you want a Hebrew nurse to look after the baby for you?" she asked.

"Yes," said the Princess. "Bring one to me," she ordered.

Moses's sister ran quickly to her mother and told her what had happened. Then she led her mother to the Princess. "Take this baby away and look after him for me. I will pay you well," said the Princess.

Moses's mother very happily took her baby son home and looked after him. He was safe now. He stayed with his mother and the rest of his family until he was old enough to go back to the Princess. Then his mother took Moses to the palace.

"He is my son now," said the Princess.

Moses grew up in the palace with the Princess. He was treated just as if he was an Egyptian prince, but he never forgot that he was really a Hebrew.

Moses Leads his People out of Egypt

Moses was an important man in Egypt, but he was very unhappy when he saw how badly the Egyptian masters treated their Hebrew slaves. One day, he saw an Egyptian whip a Hebrew man. Moses killed the Egyptian but someone saw him, and Moses knew the King would hear about it. The King would have Moses put to death.

Moses escaped into the desert and lived there for a long time. One day, he saw a bush on fire but it wasn't burning up. As he went closer, God spoke to him.

"You must go to Egypt," said God. "Take your brother Aaron with you and ask the King to let the Hebrews leave Egypt. He will not agree but I will make him. Then all the world will know that I am God. You will lead the Hebrews to a land where they will be free and have plenty to eat."

Moses didn't want to go, but he knew he must obey God. He and Aaron went to the King and asked him to set the Hebrews free.

The King was very angry. He said he wouldn't let the Hebrews go, and made them work even harder. Moses was in despair. He asked God to help him. Then he went back to the King again.

Moses warned the King that if he did not let the Hebrews leave Egypt, God would make terrible things happen. But still the King refused. Then the terrible things began. First, the river turned red and no one could drink the water.

A week later, thousands of frogs swarmed out of
the river and into all the Egyptian houses.
Then there were clouds of
horrible flies which filled
the King's palace and all
the houses, except the Hebrews' houses. But the King
wouldn't let the Hebrews go.

Then the animals began to die and the Egyptian
people were ill with horrible sores on their
bodies. After that, there were
terrible storms.

Hail flattened the crops and
great clouds of locusts ate up
what was left. But still the King
would not let the Hebrews go.

The worst thing of all was when the eldest child of every

Egyptian family died one night. God had told Moses what the Hebrews should do to be safe. Every family killed a lamb and put a little blood on the doorposts of the house. Then they roasted the lamb and ate it with flat bread and herbs. God said the Hebrews should always remember when death passed over them, and keep it as a special feast day.

At last, the King said the Hebrews could go. The next day they left Egypt, following a column of smoke during the day and a column of fire at night, sent by God.

Then the King changed his mind. He sent his army racing in chariots after the Hebrews. The Hebrews saw them coming and were terrified. In front of them was the Red Sea and behind them were the King's soldiers.

Moses told them not to be afraid because God would help them. He pointed across the water and a strong east wind, sent by God, blew away the water making a dry path for them to hurry across. But when the Egyptian soldiers tried to follow them, the sea rushed back and the soldiers were all drowned. The Hebrews were free, at last, to go to the land which God had promised them.

Moses in the Desert

Led by Moses, the people walked for weeks across the desert to their new land. They soon forgot they had been slaves in Egypt. They were hungry and grumbled. "We should have stayed in Egypt. We had plenty of food there. Remember all the good things we had to eat," they said. "We had meat and bread, melons, onions and cucumbers. It would be better to be in Egypt than dying of hunger in the desert."

God heard the people grumbling and said to Moses, "Tell the people I will give them meat to eat every evening and bread every morning."

That evening, flocks of birds, called quails, landed on the people's tents and were easy to catch. So that night everyone ate roasted quail. In the morning, the ground was covered with small white seeds. They looked just like frost. The people collected them, ground them into flour, made it into bread and baked it. They called it "manna" because it was food which came from Heaven. It was very good to eat and tasted like honey.

Every day, the same thing happened. The
people ate bread made of manna in the morning
and roasted quails in the evening. On the sixth day,
Moses told them to collect enough food for two days. This
was so they wouldn't have to work on the seventh day,
the Sabbath, but would keep it as a holy day of rest.

Now the people had plenty to eat, but soon they grew
short of water. They were thirsty and started to grumble
again. "We should have stayed in Egypt rather than die of
thirst in the desert," they said.

Moses prayed to God. "What shall I do with these people?"
he asked. "They are almost ready to kill me."

"Take your stick and walk on ahead of the people. Then
strike a rock with your stick," God said to Moses. Moses
did as God told him and when he struck the rock, a great
stream of water gushed out. There was plenty of fresh
water for everyone.

God looked after the Hebrew people all the years they
lived in the desert. He sent them food when they were
hungry and water when they were thirsty.

Moses and the Laws of God

Moses led the people across the desert to Mount Sinai, as God told him to do. For weeks they trekked across the hot, dry land but God always sent them food and water. At last, they stopped and camped at the foot of the mountain. Moses climbed up to pray to God.

God told him that the people must be ready for Him to speak to them. Then the sky grew dark, thunder rolled and lightning flashed. Smoke and fire gushed out of the top of the mountain and the ground shook. There was the sound of a loud trumpet. The people were terrified; they knew that God was near.

Then God spoke to Moses out of the fire and smoke. He gave him ten laws that the people must always keep.

"I am your God. You must have no other gods but Me.

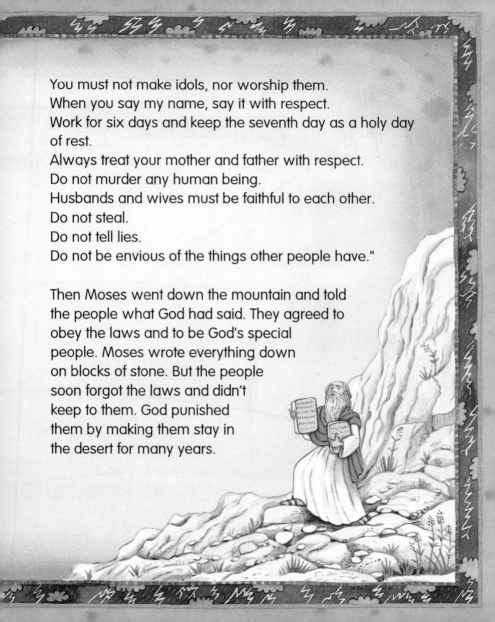

You must not make idols, nor worship them.
When you say my name, say it with respect.
Work for six days and keep the seventh day as a holy day
of rest.
Always treat your mother and father with respect.
Do not murder any human being.
Husbands and wives must be faithful to each other.
Do not steal.
Do not tell lies.
Do not be envious of the things other people have."

Then Moses went down the mountain and told
the people what God had said. They agreed to
obey the laws and to be God's special
people. Moses wrote everything down
on blocks of stone. But the people
soon forgot the laws and didn't
keep to them. God punished
them by making them stay in
the desert for many years.

Joshua and Jericho

After the people had lived for forty years in the desert, Moses died. Joshua now led the people to the land God had promised them. They crossed the Jordan river and reached the city of Jericho. God told Joshua that He would give it to them.

Joshua looked at Jericho's enormous stone walls and huge wooden gates. Then God told him what to do. Every day for six days, Joshua marched with soldiers once around the city. Behind them came seven priests who blew their trumpets. No one else made a sound.

On the seventh day, they marched around the city seven times and when the priests blew their trumpets, they all shouted as loudly as they could. Then, with a great crash, the walls fell down and the soldiers rushed into Jericho. They took all the treasure they could find. This was the people's first victory in Canaan and Joshua soon became famous. Over the years, the people settled in Canaan and grew to be a very strong nation because God was with them.

Samson, a Mighty Man

Manoah and his wife had been married for many years, but were sad because they had no children. One day, God sent an angel to Manoah's wife to tell her she would have a son. He would save her people, the Israelites, from the Philistines who ruled over them.

Manoah and his wife were delighted. When the boy was born, they called him Samson. They never cut his hair to show that he belonged to God. Samson grew up to be a huge, immensely strong man. One day, when he was walking through a vineyard, a lion roared at him. He grabbed the lion and killed it with his bare hands. Samson knew then that God had made him especially strong for the work he had to do.

He fought the Philistines whenever he could. He set fire to their crops and killed them in battles. One night, the Philistines locked Samson inside the city of Gaza.

They thought he wouldn't be able to escape and they could kill him. But Samson lifted the city gates off the gate posts and carried them away.

Samson fell in love with a beautiful Philistine girl called Delilah. The Philistines promised her a huge sum of money if she could find out why Samson was so strong. Delilah asked Samson to tell her the secret but he teased her with silly stories that weren't true.

"If you really loved me, you'd tell me the truth," she said, and asked him the question again and again. At last, Samson gave in. "My hair has never been cut," he said. "This shows I belong to God. He makes me strong."

That night, Delilah waited until Samson was fast asleep. Then she quietly called one of the Philistines who crept in

and cut off all Samson's hair. When Samson woke up, he was no stronger than any other man.

The Philistines easily captured Samson, they blinded him and tied him up with chains. Then they marched him to the city of Gaza. There they put him in prison and made him work a mill to grind grain into flour. Slowly his hair began to grow again but the Philistines didn't notice it.

One day, the Philistines held a great feast in their temple in praise of their god, Dagon. They told the people that Dagon had helped them to capture Samson. They brought Samson out of his prison so they could laugh at this huge but helpless man. They chained him between two tall pillars which held up the roof of the temple.

Samson was blind but he could feel the pillars. He asked God to give him back his strength. Then he put his huge hands against the pillars and pushed with all his might. He pushed the two pillars over, and the whole temple crashed down. Samson, all the Philistine rulers and thousands of people were killed. This was Samson's greatest show of strength. He had rescued the Israelites from their hated rulers, the Philistines.

Ruth and Naomi

Naomi grew up with her family in the town of Bethlehem but for a long time she had lived far away in Moab. Her husband and two sons had died and she shared a house with her two daughters-in-law, Orpah and Ruth. Now that she was old, Naomi longed to return to Bethlehem and her own people.

"Let us come with you," said Orpah and Ruth, and together the three women started the long journey. On the way, Naomi said, "You should stay in your own country and find new husbands." But the two girls didn't want to leave her. At last, Orpah agreed to stay in Moab but Ruth begged Naomi, "Don't make me leave you. I will go anywhere with you." So Orpah went back to Moab, and Naomi and Ruth went on to Bethlehem.

To get food, Ruth went to the fields every morning and picked up the barley the harvester had left. She ground it into flour to make bread. She didn't know the fields belonged to Naomi's rich relation, Boaz.

Boaz saw Ruth in the fields and asked who she was. When he heard how kind she had been to Naomi, he told her she would be safe in his fields and she could drink all the water she wanted from his servants' water jars.

That evening, Ruth told Naomi about Boaz. Naomi was very pleased for she knew Boaz was a good, kind man. She knew, too, that Boaz slept near his barley harvest so that it wouldn't be stolen. "Go in quietly when Boaz is asleep and lie down near his feet," Naomi said to Ruth.

When Ruth crept in, Boaz heard her. "Who's there?" he asked. "It's Ruth. I've come for your protection," she said. "There is a man who should look after you and marry you," said Boaz. "I'll talk to him tomorrow."

The next day, the man told Boaz he already had a wife. So Boaz married Ruth and, later, they had a son. Naomi was delighted, and was very happy that God had given her a grandson.

David and Goliath

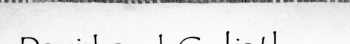

Ruth's great grandson, David, worked on his father's farm. Although he was only a young boy, he looked after his father's sheep out on the hills. He was brave and fought off the wild animals which tried to steal the sheep and lambs, even the fierce lions and bears. He led the flock over the hills to find the best grass for them. And while he watched them, he became very good at firing stones with his sling and playing his little harp.

One day, David's father asked him to take food to his three brothers who were soldiers in King Saul's army. For years King Saul had been fighting the Philistines. Now King Saul's army was camped on one side of a valley. On the other side, was the Philistine army. The two armies watched each other, not daring to attack.

One Philistine soldier was a giant of a man, called Goliath. He was tremendously strong and wore a great helmet and breastplate. He carried a huge shield and a heavy spear.

Every day, he shouted across the valley to King Saul's army, "Send one of your men to fight me. Whoever wins the fight, wins the battle for his whole army."

King Saul's army listened to Goliath's challenge but all the men were too scared to go. When David reached the army camp, he heard Goliath shouting. He said to King Saul, "I'll go and fight."

"You're only a boy. That man is a trained soldier," said King Saul.

"I'm not afraid," said David. "When I was looking after my father's sheep, I killed bears and lions with God's help. God will look after me now because Goliath wants to kill God's people."

"You may go," said King Saul, "but you must wear my fighting clothes and take my sword." David put them on but they were much too big and heavy for him. He took them off again. He picked up his shepherd's stick and chose five small stones from a stream for his sling. Then he strode down the valley to fight Goliath.

When Goliath saw David coming, he made fun of him and shouted, "Come here, boy, and I will kill you."

David walked on. "You have a sword and a spear but I have God to help me," he said. Then he put one of the little stones in his sling, swung the sling around his head, faster and faster, and let it go.

The stone shot out of the sling, straight at Goliath. It hit the giant right in the middle of his forehead. Goliath fell down on the ground. The stone had killed him. David ran up to Goliath and saw that he was dead.

When the Philistine army saw their warrior lying on the ground, they all ran away as fast as they could. King Saul's army chased them, right up to the gates of their city. The battle was over. With God's help, David had won it for them. David grew up to be a great man. He was rich with a huge family and he even became the King.

King Solomon

Solomon, the son of David, was the King of Israel. He lived in the great city of Jerusalem. One night, God came to him and asked, "What would you like me to give you?"

"I'm very young to be a ruler and have a lot to learn. I would like you to make me wise so that I can rule justly and well," said Solomon.

God was very pleased with this answer. "You could have asked to be very rich, very famous and for the death of all your enemies," said God. "But as you have asked for wisdom, I will make you the wisest man in the whole world. I will also make you very rich and famous, and you will live to be very old."

Soon King Solomon became famous for his wise judgements and people came to listen to the many wise things he said.

One day, two women came to his court to ask for his help.

The first woman said, "This woman and I live in the same house. A few days ago, we both gave birth to babies. This woman's baby died, but she stole my baby and now says that it is hers."

"No, your baby died," screamed the second woman. "This baby is mine. I can tell it is my child."

"Bring me my sword," King Solomon ordered one of his guards. When the man brought it, King Solomon said, "Now, cut the baby in half and give one half to each of these women."

One of the women shouted, "Yes, kill the baby and then neither of us can have it." But the other woman cried, "My Lord, please do not kill the child. Give it to this woman and let it live."

King Solomon knew then that this was really the mother and gave her the baby.

Solomon and his Temple

Solomon had been King for four years when he began to build a Temple where he could worship God. Hundreds of men dug out stone from quarries in the hills and cut it into exactly the right shapes for the foundations and walls. Solomon wanted cedar wood to line the walls. The best cedar trees grew to the north where the land was ruled by King Hiram of Tyre.

King Solomon made a treaty with King Hiram. Hiram agreed to have the trees cut down and float the logs down the coast to the Temple. In return, Solomon sent huge amounts of wheat and oil to Hiram every year.

Thousands of men worked on the Temple. There were two rooms. The inside room was square with no windows. This was the most sacred part. Only the

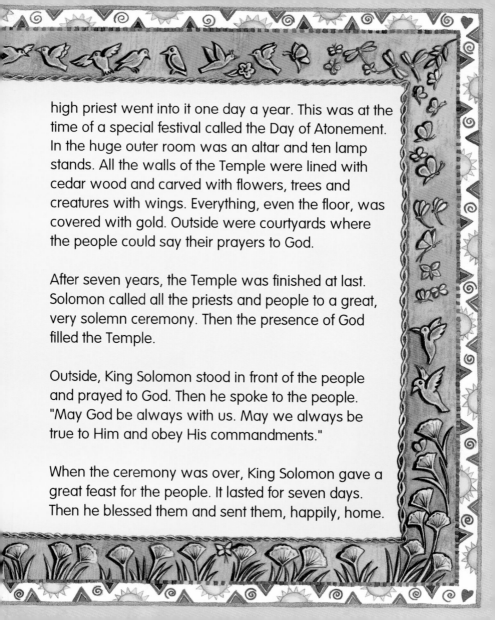

high priest went into it one day a year. This was at the time of a special festival called the Day of Atonement. In the huge outer room was an altar and ten lamp stands. All the walls of the Temple were lined with cedar wood and carved with flowers, trees and creatures with wings. Everything, even the floor, was covered with gold. Outside were courtyards where the people could say their prayers to God.

After seven years, the Temple was finished at last. Solomon called all the priests and people to a great, very solemn ceremony. Then the presence of God filled the Temple.

Outside, King Solomon stood in front of the people and prayed to God. Then he spoke to the people. "May God be always with us. May we always be true to Him and obey His commandments."

When the ceremony was over, King Solomon gave a great feast for the people. It lasted for seven days. Then he blessed them and sent them, happily, home.

Elijah

Elijah lived in Israel and loved and obeyed God. The new King of Israel had built a huge temple to a false god, called Baal, and his Queen was wicked and cruel. Many of the people followed their King and forgot about God. Elijah warned them that there would be no rain for many years and they would starve.

God said to Elijah, "Go to the Kerith valley and live there in safety. You can drink water from the stream and ravens will bring you food."

Elijah did as God told him and every morning and evening the ravens brought him bread and meat, and he drank water from the stream.

But, after a while,
the stream dried up
because there was no
rain. Then God told him to go
to the city of Sidon where a
woman would give him food.

There Elijah met a woman picking up a few
sticks for her fire. "Please give me a drink
of water and some bread," said Elijah.
"I have no food," said the
woman. "All I have is a
little flour and a few
drops of olive oil. I'm
going to bake one
loaf over a fire of

these sticks. When we have eaten the loaf, my son and I will starve to death."

"Go home," said Elijah, "and bake a small loaf for me and one for you and your son. From now on, you'll find that your flour and oil for bread will never run out."

The woman did what Elijah told her and found that every day she always had just enough flour and oil to make bread. But, one day, the woman's son became very ill and died. The woman was heartbroken. "Why have you killed my son?" she asked Elijah. "Is it to punish me for the wrong things I've done in my life?"

"Give the boy to me," said Elijah. He carried the boy upstairs and laid him on his bed. There he prayed three times to God, "Please bring this boy back to life."

God answered Elijah's prayer. The boy sat up, alive and well. Elijah picked him up and carried him down to his mother. "Look," he said, "your son is alive." The woman was overjoyed. "I know now that you are a man of God and what you say is true," she said.

Elisha and Naaman

Naaman was the commander of the Syrian army. He was a brave soldier and a rich man with a big house and lots of servants, but he had a horrible skin disease, called leprosy.

Naaman's wife had a new slave. She was a young girl who had been captured by the Syrians during a raid on Israel. She said to Naaman's wife, "If lord Naaman could go to the prophet Elisha in Israel, I know he would be cured of his disease."

When Naaman was told what the slave had said, he went to the King of Syria. The King gave Naaman leave to go to Israel and gave him a letter for the King of Israel. Naaman rode off in his chariot with his servants, taking gifts of silver and gold, and clothes for Elisha. When he reached Elisha's house, a servant came to the door.

"My master says that you must go to the Jordan and

wash in the river seven times," said the servant. "Then you will be cured."

Naaman was very angry. "Why won't Elisha come out to see me?" he shouted. "I thought he'd call on his God and I'd be cured. And why must I wash in the Jordan? There are lots of much better rivers in Syria."

He started to drive away in his chariot but one of his servants stopped him. "My master," said the servant, "if Elisha had asked you to do something difficult, you would have done it. As he only says you should wash in the Jordan, shouldn't you try it?"

Namaan realized that the servant was right. He went to the Jordan and washed in it seven times. When he walked out of the river, his skin was clear and smooth. He was cured of the disease.

Delighted, he rushed back to Elisha to thank him. "I know now," said Naaman, "that there is only one true God." He tried to give Elisha all the gifts he had brought from Syria but Elisha wouldn't take them. He blessed Naaman and sent him home.

Daniel and the Lions

Daniel was only a boy when Jerusalem was captured by the Babylonians. He was taken, with other people, to the magnificent city of Babylon. There he and other boys were given plenty of tasty food, a good schooling, and were taken care of. But Daniel never forgot he came from Israel, and he prayed to God three times every day.

Daniel grew up strong and wise. When King Darius ruled Babylon, he made Daniel one of the three rulers of the whole kingdom. The other two rulers were jealous of Daniel and plotted to get rid of him. But they couldn't find that Daniel had done anything wrong.

In the end, they went to King Darius. "Make a new law, O King," they said. "For thirty days everyone must pray only to you. If anyone prays to any god, they shall be fed to the lions." The King made the law.

Daniel heard about the law but three times every day he still knelt at his window to say his prayers to God.

The two rulers watched and then went off to report him to the King.

The King was very upset. He liked and trusted Daniel but he couldn't save him from the law. He ordered Daniel to be put into the lion pit. As Daniel walked down into it, and the entrance was closed up with a huge stone, the King said "May your God save you."

King Darius went back to his palace. That night, he was so upset, he couldn't eat any supper. He sent his servants away and couldn't sleep. Early the next morning, he went to the lion pit. "Did your God save you?" he shouted to Daniel. "I am here," answered Daniel. "God kept the lions' mouths shut. He knows I've done nothing wrong."

The King was delighted that Daniel was safe. He ordered him to be taken out of the pit. Then he ordered the two rulers to be put into the pit with the lions.

The King made a new law. He ordered that everyone in his kingdom should respect Daniel's God, the God who had saved Daniel from the lions.

Brave Esther

King Xerxes was rich and powerful and ruled the huge Persian empire. After he had been king for three years, he gave a magnificent feast which lasted for seven days. Thousands of guests were served the most delicious food and drank the best wines out of golden cups.

One night, he said to one of his servants, "Bring Queen Vashti here to me." He wanted everyone to see how beautiful his queen was. But Queen Vashti was holding her own feast and sent a message saying that she wouldn't come. King Xerxes was furious with her. He ordered her out of his palace and announced that she was no longer his wife.

King Xerxes wanted a new queen. He sent his servants all over his kingdom to find the most beautiful girls so that he could choose one for his new wife.

A man called Mordecai worked in King Xerxes' palace. He was from Jerusalem. He had a young cousin, called

Esther, whom he had brought up as his own daughter because her father and mother were dead. She was a beautiful girl who was always sweet-tempered and kind.

When King Xerxes looked at the girls brought from all over his kingdom, he chose Esther to be his new wife. Soon she was crowned Queen Esther. But Mordecai warned her many times never to tell anyone she was a Hebrew and not a Persian girl.

One day, Mordecai heard two men whispering together. They were plotting to kill King Xerxes. "You must warn your husband," Mordecai said to Esther and told her who these men were. Esther told the King, who had the two men put to death. He was very pleased that Esther and Mordecai were loyal to him.

The King's chief of staff was a proud and cruel man called Haman. Everyone had to bow to him but Mordecai would not bow. "I am a Jew. My people and I bow only to God," he said. Haman was very angry. He told the King that some people were making trouble in his kingdom. The King said he should deal with them in any way he liked. Haman ordered that Mordecai and all the Jewish people be killed on a certain day. No one knew that Queen Esther was also a Jew.

When Esther heard the news, she was very upset. Mordecai said to her, "You must go to the King and beg him to save the lives of your people."

"I can't do that," Esther replied. "I always have to wait for the King to send for me. If I go to him, he may be angry and have me killed."

"God may have made you the Queen so that you can save us," said Mordecai.

Esther was terrified but she went to the King. Haman was there with him. She invited both of them to dinner the next day. The King was very pleased and Haman felt very proud to be dining with the King and Queen. But then he thought of Mordecai and how the Jew would not bow to him. Very angry, he ordered that Mordecai should be hung the next morning.

That night King Xerxes could not sleep. Reading through the palace records, he came across Mordecai's name and remembered that Mordecai had saved his life. "I must reward him," said King Xerxes. So, instead of being hanged in the morning, Mordecai was rewarded by the King who ordered he should be given rich clothes and a fine horse.

When King Xerxes and Haman went to dine with Esther the next day, Esther begged the King for a kindness. The King looked at his beautiful wife. "You may have anything you wish for. You only have to ask," he said.

"I and all my people are to be killed," Esther said. "Please will you save us?" The King was horrified. "Who dared to give the order for this?" he demanded. "It was Haman," said Esther.

Haman knelt in front of Esther and begged her to save him, but King Xerxes ordered him to be hanged. Then the King ordered that all the Jewish people in his kingdom were not to be killed, but were to be treated well and with respect. Esther had saved her people from death.

Jonah and the Whale

Jonah was a good man who usually did what God told him. But one day, God told Jonah to go to the city of Nineveh. He was to tell the people there that God had seen that they were very bad and would punish them.

Jonah didn't want to go. Instead, he ran away to the port at Joppa and found a ship that was going to Tarshish, a very long way from Nineveh. He thought God wouldn't be able to see him there. He paid his fare and went on board the ship.

As soon as it sailed off across the sea, there was a huge storm. It had been sent by God. The sailors were terrified and threw everything overboard to make the ship lighter because it was in danger of sinking. The captain told them to pray to their gods to save them.

All through the storm, Jonah lay fast asleep in the bottom of the ship. The captain went to Jonah and shook him to wake him up. "You must pray too," he shouted.

"I can't pray to God," Jonah shouted back. "I'm running away from Him."

The sailors thought Jonah had brought the storm and they would all die. They begged him to tell them how to make the water calm. "You must throw me in the sea," said Jonah. But the captain told the sailors, "I can't kill this man."

"You must," said Jonah. "You'll die unless you throw me overboard. Then the storm will stop." The storm grew worse and worse and, at last, the captain agreed.

The sailors threw Jonah into the sea and, at once, the storm was over. The sailors thanked Jonah's God for saving their lives.

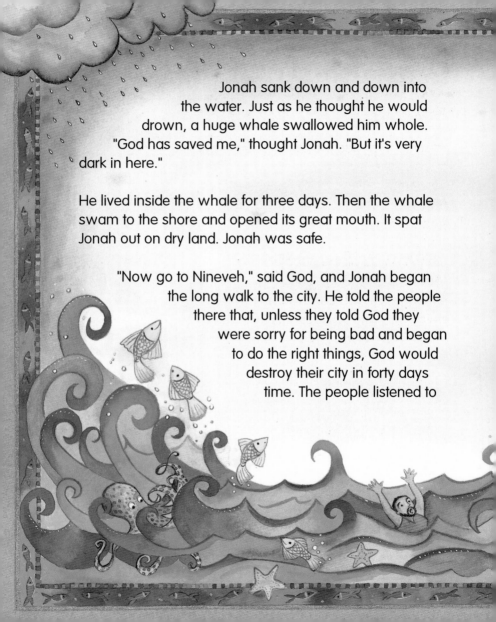

Jonah sank down and down into the water. Just as he thought he would drown, a huge whale swallowed him whole. "God has saved me," thought Jonah. "But it's very dark in here."

He lived inside the whale for three days. Then the whale swam to the shore and opened its great mouth. It spat Jonah out on dry land. Jonah was safe.

"Now go to Nineveh," said God, and Jonah began the long walk to the city. He told the people there that, unless they told God they were sorry for being bad and began to do the right things, God would destroy their city in forty days time. The people listened to

Jonah and the King ordered them to be sorry for their badness and pray to God.

Jonah sat outside the city and waited for it to be destroyed. He was very hot and very cross. He wanted God to destroy Nineveh. But God saw that the people had turned to Him and He saved the city.

"Jonah, I love all the people in Nineveh," said God, "and I am everywhere. You can't run away from me." And Jonah knew that this was true.